Keep 'em Reading
BOOK REPORTS

12 Engaging, Hands-on Activities

Sara M. Orme

UpstartBooks

Fort Atkinson, Wisconsin

To my dad, a lifetime educator. Thanks.

Published by **UpstartBooks**
W5527 Highway 106
P.O. Box 800
Fort Atkinson, Wisconsin 53538-0800
1-800-448-4887

© Sara M. Orme, 2002
Cover design: Heidi Green, illustration by Ben De Soto

The paper used in this publication meets the minimum requirements of American National Standard for Information Science—Permanence of Paper for Printed Library Material. ANSI/NISO Z39.48-1992.

Contents

Introduction

When students are given a book report assignment, they usually respond with:

- "Awww … do we have to?" (Means: it's boring.)

- "I just read a book and now I have to write about it!?" (Means: it's hard and discouraging.)

So why do teachers ask students to write book reports? Because they want evidence that their students have read the book and because book reports are a good writing exercise. Library media specialists might ask students to write book reports for the same reasons. But book reports are also a practical way to encourage library use, teach library skills, foster an appreciation of literature and enrich students' reading experiences.

In typical book reports students recount the events of the story, but don't interact with the characters or the plot in any other way. Nor do they produce a work that is new, "belongs" to the student or is even very interesting. This kind of report requires little thinking to challenge gifted students and can be downright discouraging for struggling students. And let's face it, they're not much fun for the student to write or for the teacher to read. Who wants to read 38 summaries of Goosebumps Volume #1?

Keep 'em Reading Book Reports **is designed for grades 3 and up and contains activities that:**

- are fun to do and fun to grade

- prove without a doubt that students have read the books

- are difficult to plagiarize

- challenge and occupy gifted students

- empower struggling students and showcase their strengths

- excite students to share what they have been reading

The activities in this book require reading and writing skills, the two legs on which language arts stands. But they also require intelligences and higher level thinking skills. For this reason, the activities will appeal to the whole spectrum of students. Children who typically struggle in language arts can excel with these activities and work on their reading and writing skills at the same time. Successful and gifted students will be able to experiment with creative expression, beyond reporting back simple facts. All students will be able to highlight their strengths and exercise their weaknesses.

Background & Philosophy

Everyone who works in a classroom knows that all students are not alike. They have different skills and abilities. They excel in different areas. Different things make them tick. Different forces motivate them. According to Howard Gardner, award-winning educator and author, part of the reason for these differences is that people are created with multiple intelligences.

Schoolwork typically focuses on linguistic intelligence—the ability to learn and communicate what you know through words, most often the written word. Other intelligences include:

- math/logical—the ability to relate separate pieces of information to each other, to use symbols well and to reason deductively and inductively

- kinesthetic—the ability to do or act and to think better while moving

- spatial—the ability to think in pictures and to use visual resources well

- musical—the ability to use sounds and rhythms and to learn things set to music quickly

- interpersonal—the ability to work with others, communicate effectively and seek relationships

- intrapersonal—the ability to work independently and analyze one's own thinking

Because schools tend to emphasize verbal skills, linguistically weak students often struggle in the classroom. The boy who is reading a grade level or two behind, but who can take apart and reassemble his father's lawnmower without instructions is an intelligent young man—kinesthetically, spatially and logically. Ask him to write a typical book report and he will struggle, become discouraged and likely fail the assignment. But ask him to interact with the book by creating something with his hands or acting out a scene and he will be excited, creative and motivated! A motivated student learns; a discouraged student does not.

The idea behind the activities in this book is to highlight the students' strengths and exercise their weaknesses. Does that mean the boy should never be asked to write in school? No, he still needs to build up his weaker skills. But he should have the chance to use his strengths to learn, show what he has learned and succeed in school. Reading and writing are the legs that language arts stands on, but the spatial arms and the kinesthetic knees need to exercise themselves once in a while.

In the same regard, brains atrophy when the only kind of exercise they get is to shelve information and retrieve it only occasionally. Too often this is all that students' brains are asked to do. The activities in this book require the higher level thinking skills that are based on Benjamin Bloom's Taxonomy of Cognitive Processes. They will challenge all students by asking them to look at a novel in its parts (analysis), create something new from what they have read (synthesis), apply what they have learned (application) and make judgments (evaluation). That is much more interesting than simply reporting back the events of the novel.

With this resource in hand, you can take a different approach to book reports. Get all of your students excited to share what they have been reading by providing them with opportunities for success. Success in this area will spread throughout a student's education and across the curriculum. It can start with you.

How to Use This Book

The activities in this book can be used in a variety of ways. They are designed for use with chapter books, but they will also work with many short stories. You can determine the best way to use the activities based on your objectives, time frame and curriculum. The activities can be:

- ready for class use without additional preparation

- kept on file for a last minute time-filler or take-home extra credit

- used in place of a test or quiz

- used to review a literary term

- used as a quick review of a book read by the whole class

- used in collaboration with classroom assignments and units

- assigned following a booktalk, for students to complete after reading the book

The Independent Study Unit

These activities can also be used as an independent study unit that lasts approximately one month. Students choose a novel and complete a packet of activities at their own pace. The teacher or librarian acts as a consultant as the students encounter problems or questions.

Procedure:

- Each student chooses a chapter book of a specified length, such as 150 pages.

- The teacher/librarian provides independent reading class periods over a few weeks.

- The teacher/librarian prepares a packet for each student by photocopying some or all of the reproducibles in this book and stapling them together with a blank sheet on top. The blank sheet is for the student to create a Cover Sheet.

- After completing their books, the students receive the prepared packet of activities.

- The students complete the packets over the next week or two of class time. Anything not finished during class time should be done as homework.

- The teacher/librarian sets aside one class period at the end of the unit for students to present their best work (i.e., perform reader's theater scripts, exchange rebus puzzles, etc.).

- The teacher/librarian collects, grades and displays the packets.

Grading the Packet:

I recommend grading the packet by giving each page an individual grade with an additional grade for neatness/spelling/use of color. For example, the 12 activities might be worth 10 points each and neatness/spelling/use of color might be worth 10 points, for a total of 130 points. If the activity packet is used in place of a test or as the culminating activity for a unit, the point total should equal a test grade. Because of the varying skills and intelligences used with these activities, students may do very well on some and not as well on others. Therefore it is better for them and easier for you to grade each activity separately. Assigning 10 points per activity makes it easy to assess each one as an A (10 or 9 points), B (8 points), C (7 points), etc.

Using Color

I recommend that students be required to use color, preferably colored pencils, to highlight their activity sheets. This does not mean that students have to draw illustrations (unless stated in the instructions), but they should color in the headings, special words or anything else they like. Illustrations or designs may be added if the student wishes.

Using color is deliberate and requires care. When students choose colors and apply them to their activities they become more aware of the presentation of their work and they take more pride in the outcome. It is hard to be haphazard about writing on paper that you have taken the time to decorate. Some students will even complete the packet in pencil first and then go back over everything in ink so they don't make any permanent mistakes.

The Activities

This section contains the 12 activities with reproducibles. Each includes a statement of purpose, the thinking skills and intelligences involved, an overview, directions for the students and notes for the teacher or librarian. If you choose to use these activities as an Independent Study Unit as described on page 7, have the students make cover sheets for their packets.

Cover Sheet

Purpose: To identify book, author and student when used as an independent study unit.

Intelligences: linguistic, spatial

Thinking Skills: knowledge

Directions to Students: Use a blank sheet of paper to create a cover for your booklet. Include the title, author's name, your name (and class period if desired), due date and a colored illustration or design.

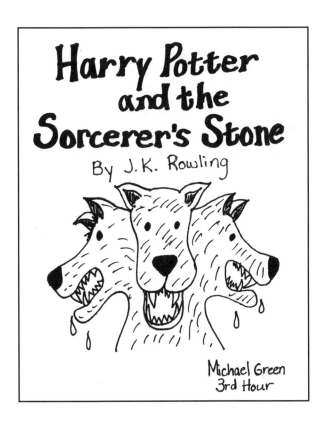

Map Making

Purpose: To encourage students to visualize setting and to turn words into pictures.

Intelligences: spatial, math/logical (geometry)

Thinking Skills: knowledge, comprehension, application, synthesis

About the Activity: Making a map of the setting(s) in a novel requires students to visualize the author's descriptive passages, allows spatially and logically gifted students to shine and forces students struggling in spatial and logical intelligences to further develop their skills.

While a map can be an artistic piece, it is not necessary in this assignment. Students who feel that they can't draw should not be intimidated. Buildings and geographic features can be represented by symbols such as rectangles and triangles. Students who wish to draw detailed, realistic representations may do so. Either way, students should draw neatly and use color.

Directions to Students: Draw a map of the setting or one of the settings in your novel. Re-read descriptive passages if necessary. Be sure to use color.

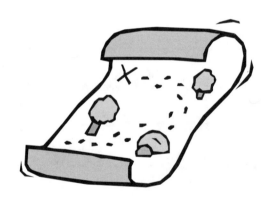

Map Making

Draw a map of the setting or one of the settings in your novel.
Re-read descriptive passages if necessary. Be sure to use color.

Pyramid Poems

Purpose: To review parts of speech and highlight character.

Intelligences: linguistic, math/logical (patterns)

Thinking Skills: knowledge, comprehension, application

About the Activity: A pyramid poem follows a set pattern which contains a certain number of words and parts of speech in each line. The poems are an alternative to the typical paragraph character description and demonstrate what the students know about the main characters in the books they have read. The poems are also a good opportunity to review adjectives, verbs and synonyms.

Here is a sample poem about Santa Claus:

Santa	*name*
fat old	*two physical adjectives*
jolly kind generous	*three personality adjectives*
descends eats delivers ascends	*four verbs*
brings presents to good children	*five-word phrase*
St. Nick	*synonym for line one*

Directions to Students: Write two pyramid poems about different characters from your novel. One poem should be about the main character and the other poem should be about a supporting character. A pyramid poem has six lines with the following pattern:

name of character
two adjectives that describe the physical appearance of the character
three adjectives that describe the personality of the character
four verbs or actions the character does
a five-word phrase about the character
a synonym (or another name) for the character

Notes to Teacher:

- You might want to practice writing a pyramid poem together. Use a character from a book the class has already read or from a familiar fairy tale or story.

- You can use this activity to teach or review protagonist and antagonist by requiring that the pyramid poems be about these two characters.

Pyramid Poems

Write two pyramid poems about different characters from your novel using the pattern below. One poem should be about the main character and the other poem should be about a supporting character.

1

_____
name

_____ _____
two physical adjectives

_____ _____ _____
three personality adjectives

_____ _____ _____ _____
four verbs

_____ _____ _____ _____ _____
a five-word phrase

_____
synonym for line one

2

_____
name

_____ _____
two physical adjectives

_____ _____ _____
three personality adjectives

_____ _____ _____ _____
four verbs

_____ _____ _____ _____ _____
a five-word phrase

_____
synonym for line one

Twenty Questions

Purpose: To encourage students to think beyond what the author states about the plot and characters.

Intelligences: linguistic, interpersonal

Thinking Skills: analysis, evaluation

About the Activity: Remember the Twenty Questions game that helped you pass the time on long car trips? This activity is the same idea. When students create 20 questions to "ask" the characters in their books, they start to think of the characters as real people. This is an important thing for students to understand when they write stories of their own. In addition, writing only yes or no questions exercises the students' evaluation skills. They must evaluate their own questions and determine if they can be answered with yes or no. This is difficult for some younger students, but they become more proficient with practice.

Directions to Students: Write 20 yes or no questions that you would like to ask the main character. They can be about what happened in the story or help you get to know the character better.

Notes to Teacher: You might play Twenty Questions as a class. This would introduce the game to students who have never played and get students thinking of yes or no questions. Students can play in pairs or the whole class can work together to guess what the teacher is thinking.

20 Questions

...Hmmm

Write 20 yes or no questions that you would like to ask the main character. They can be about what happened in the story or help you get to know the character better.

1. _____
2. _____
3. _____
4. _____
5. _____
6. _____
7. _____
8. _____
9. _____
10. _____
11. _____
12. _____
13. _____
14. _____
15. _____
16. _____
17. _____
18. _____
19. _____
20. _____

Story in Song

Purpose: To summarize the plot in a non-traditional way.

Intelligences: musical, linguistic

Thinking Skills: knowledge, comprehension, synthesis

About the Activity: This activity is fun, but also a challenge to many students. It is amusing to watch a classroom full of heads bobbing, toes tapping and fingers dancing as students strive to write new lyrics to well-known melodies. The idea is to tell the plot of a novel by setting it to music. Bonus points go to those interpersonal performers who will also sing their songs for the class.

Directions to Students: Choose a well-known tune such as "Twinkle, Twinkle, Little Star" and compose at least two verses that summarize the plot of your novel.

Notes to Teacher:

- Stress choosing a well-known melody, not something from the recent pop charts. You will want to be able to recognize the tune as you grade the activity.

- Give students the opportunity for performance. It will be easier for some students to share their songs if they can teach it to a few friends and sing it together.

- After grading this activity, it is fun to make a bulletin board of songs. Students enjoy reading the songs and trying to sing them.

Retell a Story in a Song

Choose a well-known tune such as "Twinkle, Twinkle, Little Star" and compose at least two verses that summarize the plot of your novel.

Tune: _____

Pen Pal

Purpose: To role play the character and extend the action of the novel. This activity may focus on theme.

Intelligences: linguistic, interpersonal

Thinking Skills: comprehension, application, analysis, synthesis

About the Activity: Writing letters is a familiar activity for most students. Many middle school students write letters to friends they see daily—what teacher hasn't caught students passing notes? A teaching maxim says, "When introducing new skills, use familiar content and when introducing new content, use familiar skills." The familiar format of letter writing is a comfortable way for students to express the theme of a novel and it is often a new literary concept for this age.

The student can role play the character and write a letter recounting part of the plot, adding to the plot, describing the setting or telling about himself or herself. These letters can be written to another character, the student or class, the character's diary, etc. They should be signed in the character's name.

Alternatively, you can teach theme, then have the students write a letter from the main character that will discuss the lessons he or she learned during the course of the novel. Or have the student role play the character and use the letter to express what they think the author was trying to get across.

Directions to Students: Write a _____ paragraph letter from the main character to _____ about _____. Sign the letter with the character's name.

Notes to Teacher: Encourage students who want to decorate or illustrate their letter.

LETTER FROM MAIN CHARACTER

Date:

Dear _____,

Signed, _____

Rebus

Purpose: To describe setting or character using symbols.

Intelligences: spatial (symbolic), linguistic, math/logical

Thinking Skills: comprehension, application, analysis, synthesis

About the Activity: A rebus is a puzzle that uses both words and pictures to write sentences. The classic 👁 ♡ U meaning "I love you," is one example. More complex rebuses use arithmetic symbols to add or subtract letters and sounds from representations of words. For example: 🚌 – B would be "us" from the symbol "bus" minus the "b" sound.

This activity is challenging for many students because it forces them to think in new ways and requires multiple skills. But it is also fun to make a puzzle, especially if the students will eventually exchange papers and solve each others' rebuses. Creating a rebus requires students to use visual, symbolic and linguistic skills. They must consider:

- How does this word look?

- How does it sound?

- How do I represent this word so other people can decipher it?

There is also the challenge of actually drawing the rebus—another chance for some students to shine and others to build up their weaker skills.

Directions to Students: Create three rebus sentences that describe the setting or characters in your novel. Use both words and pictures.

Notes to Teacher:

- When you introduce this assignment you will want to draw examples on the board and perhaps create rebus sentences as a class.

- For your convenience, you may want to require students to write out the solutions to their puzzles. They can do this on another sheet of paper or upside down at the bottom of the worksheet.

- This activity is fun to post on a bulletin board or circulate in class so students can solve each others' puzzles.

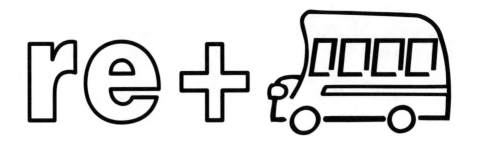

Create three rebus sentences that describe the setting or characters in your novel. Use both words and pictures.

Example:

(I think you are great!)

Reader's Theater

Purpose: To practice writing dialogue (with optional public speaking or acting opportunity).

Intelligences: linguistic, interpersonal, kinesthetic (if performed)

Thinking Skills: comprehension, application, analysis, synthesis, evaluation

About the Activity: Reader's theater is a dramatic reading of a literary work. Old-time radio serials are examples of reader's theater with added music and sound effects. Of course, with minor changes, most reader's theater scripts can also be acted.

For this activity students write one scene from the novel as a reader's theater script. They must decide:

- The essential elements of a scene that must be included to convey the scene to a listening audience.

- If a narrator will be required. If so, what kind of information does the narrator need to share? What can be accomplished through dialogue alone?

- Where the script should start and stop.

Interpersonal and kinesthetic types will want to perform their scripts with the help of their friends. Some will want to read their scripts, perhaps with music or sound effects, and others will want to act them out. These are wonderful bonus activities for both the performers and the audience. Other students may be piqued to read the book from watching or listening to the selected scene and—I keep saying it—it's just fun!

Directions to Students: Write a reader's theater script (at least one page in length) based on an important scene in your novel. It helps to have a narrator who can set up the scene and inform the audience of the plot.

Notes to Teacher:

- Require the script to be written, not just performed. Performance is a bonus or extra credit activity.

- Plan a reader's theater period or partial period for those who wish to perform their scripts. You might serve refreshments and ask the students to dress up for the event as if they were going to a real theater.

Reader's Theater

Write a script based on an important scene in your novel. It helps to have a narrator who can set up the scene and inform your audience of the plot.

Conflict Collage

Purpose: To highlight conflict.

Intelligences: spatial, linguistic

Thinking Skills: knowledge, comprehension, application, analysis, synthesis

About the Activity: A collage is artwork made up of many images layered together. The images are usually found, rather than drawn, and words can be used. In this collage activity, students will analyze their novels for the five classic types of conflict:

- Person vs. Person
- Person vs. Nature
- Person vs. Society
- Person vs. God/Supernatural (Fate)
- Person vs. Self

Once the students have determined the types of conflict in their novels, they will look for words and images from magazines, newspapers, etc., that depict the conflict(s).

Students should not feel that they need to represent the specific characters or conflict from their books, only the same type of conflict. For example, a student who reads *Call of the Wild* and wants to show Person vs. Person (or in this case Animal vs. Animal) could show any two animals fighting; they do not need to be dogs. This is another activity that takes the pressure off the student who does not excel at writing, but accurately shows if he or she understands conflict.

Directions to Students: Create a collage using found words and pictures that illustrate the type(s) of conflict in your novel.

Notes to Teacher:

- It is helpful to review the types of conflict before beginning the assignment.
- Try to have a variety of magazines for students on hand. Ask parents to donate any they might have.
- Encourage students to find other sources for pictures such as computer graphics programs or used books.

Conflict COLLAGE

Create a collage using found words and pictures that illustrate the type(s) of conflict in your novel.

Evaluate the Ending

Purpose: To evaluate and express opinions with supporting reasons.

Intelligences: linguistic, intrapersonal

Thinking Skills: evaluation

About the Activity: This activity is a chance for students to express whether they liked or disliked their books. However, when asked to evaluate a work, whether it be a movie, novel or another student's paper, students often have trouble getting past, "I liked it," "It was good" or "I didn't like it very much."

This activity has some guiding questions to help avoid such succinct answers and to get students to explain why they feel the way they do.

Directions to Students: Rate your book on a scale of 1 to 10 (10 is the best). Then answer the questions on the worksheet.

Notes to Teacher: Make a bulletin board display with the ranking of the books. Give each student a strip of colored paper. Have the students write the title of their book on the paper strip (as if it was the spine of a book) and the ranking they chose. Pin the strips to the board so they look like a shelf of books—start with the highest ranked books at one end, down to the lower ranked books. Students can easily see what books their peers do and don't recommend. Some books may even appear at both ends of the bookshelf!

Evaluate the Ending

Rate your book on a scale of 1 to 10 (10 is the best). Then answer the questions below.

Did the book satisfy you? Why or why not?

As the author, what would you do differently?

Rating (circle one)

WORST 1 2 3 4 5 6 7 8 9 10 BEST

Word Search

Purpose: To present plot events to others in the form of a game.

Intelligences: linguistic, math/logical

Thinking Skills: application, synthesis

About the Activity: Word searches are popular games with kids and adults alike. With this activity, students can create their own word searches based on the plot of their novel or story. Each student thinks of 12 plot events that can be summed up in one or two words (such as "party" or "basketball game"), writes out explanations or clues for the events and creates the word search grid by filling in the extra squares on the reproducible.

Individual Books: If this activity is done with books that the students have read independently, the students should list each word with a sentence explaining what the word has to do with the book. This helps someone completing the puzzle find out about the book and it shows the teacher or librarian that the student didn't just pick the words out of thin air!

Class Book: When the entire class has read the same book, the students should write clues that must be solved and create a word bank. This shows the knowledge of the student creating the puzzle and tests the knowledge of the students completing it.

Directions to Students: Create a word search by choosing 12 events from the book. Write a one-sentence clue or explanation for each word. Write your words in the grid, then fill in the extra spaces with other letters. Use all capital letters.

Notes to Teacher: This is another good activity for sharing.

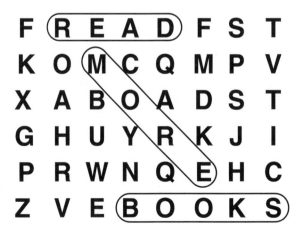

Word Search

Create a word search by choosing 12 events from your book. Write a one-sentence clue or explanation for each word. Write your words in the grid, then fill in the extra spaces with other letters. Use all capital letters.

Title: _____

Author: _____

1. _____
2. _____
3. _____
4. _____
5. _____
6. _____
7. _____
8. _____
9. _____
10. _____
11. _____
12. _____

Fortunately/Unfortunately

Purpose: To recount plot events.

Intelligences: linguistic, math/logical

Thinking Skills: application, analysis, evaluation

About the Activity: In this activity, students recall the plot events in order and determine if the events are fortunate or unfortunate. Next, they write and illustrate a comic strip, alternating good and bad events that begin with "Fortunately, …" or "Unfortunately, …"

Here is an example using *Goldilocks and the Three Bears:*

Mama Bear made a big pot of porridge.

The bear family was hungry.

Fortunately, Mama Bear made a big pot of porridge.

Unfortunately, it was too hot to eat.

Fortunately, they could take a nice walk while it cooled.

Unfortunately, a hungry Goldilocks entered their house.

Fortunately, she ate some food.

Unfortunately, she broke Baby Bear's chair.

Fortunately, she found a bed in which to rest.

Unfortunately, the bears discovered her in the bed.

Fortunately, she escaped and never returned to the forest.

Directions to Students: Create a Fortunately/Unfortunately comic strip with events from your book. Begin with a statement from the beginning of the story. Follow with a sentence about the next event. Write Fortunately or Unfortunately (whichever is appropriate)at the top of the box. Then draw a picture that goes with that sentence. Continue, alternating Fortunate and Unfortunate events.

Notes to Teacher:

- To begin, read the example above to the class. If you like, use a well-known tale to create a Fortunately/Unfortunately story as a class. You can also enlarge the illustration above to show the students how to get started.

- Most stories have many "fortunate" and "unfortunate" events, but this activity may not work for all.

- This activity is another good bulletin board idea.

FORTUNATELY
UNFORTUNATELY

Create a Fortunately/Unfortunately comic strip with events from your book. Begin with a statement from the beginning of the story. Follow with a sentence about the next event. Write Fortunately or Unfortunately (whichever is appropriate)at the top of the box. Then draw a picture that goes with that sentence. Continue, alternating Fortunate and Unfortunate events.

Start: _____

Write beginning statement here.

Design a Back Cover

Purpose: To complete a "real world" writing and design task.

Intelligences: linguistic, interpersonal, intrapersonal, spatial

Thinking Skills: comprehension, analysis, application, synthesis, evaluation

About the Activity: Most of us check the back covers of books when we are browsing for a good read. And most back covers provide the browser with an introduction to the protagonist, a taste of the plot and a dose of suspense, all designed to create a desire to find out more.

By asking students to create a back cover that will entice other students to read their books, you are giving them a writing task with a specific audience and purpose. The students need to analyze their audience to determine what will pique their interest in a book. They need to evaluate what they have read to determine what will create the suspense and interest that will excite their peers. Incidentally, this activity is also "real world" writing—the kind that marketers do. Some students may find that it is something they enjoy and want to pursue as a career.

The project becomes interpersonal when students create reviews by interviewing classmates who have read the same book. They could also include reviews that they made up themselves.

Illustrations may be included.

Directions to Students: Create a back cover for the novel that will entice other students to read it. Write a short description of the book that creates suspense and interest. You may include reviews (comments people have made about the book) and illustrations. Use color. The cover you design does not have to be like the real back cover of the book.

Notes to Teacher: This activity is another good bulletin board idea.

Design a Back Cover

Create a back cover for your book that will entice other students to read it. Write a short description that creates suspense and interest. You may include reviews (comments people have made about the book) and illustrations. Don't forget to use color.

Intelligences and Thinking Skills Matrix

	Linguistic	Math/Logical	Kinesthetic	Spatial	Musical	Interpersonal	Intrapersonal	Knowledge	Comprehension	Application	Analysis	Synthesis	Evaluation
Cover Sheet	●			●				●					
Map Making		●		●				●	●	●		●	
Pyramid Poems	●	●						●	●	●			
Twenty Questions	●					●					●		●
Story in Song	●				●			●	●			●	
Pen Pal	●					●			●	●	●	●	
Rebus	●	●		●					●	●	●	●	
Reader's Theater	●		●			●			●	●	●	●	●
Conflict Collage	●			●				●	●	●	●	●	
Evaluate the Ending	●						●						●
Word Search	●	●								●		●	
Fortunately/ Unfortunately	●	●								●	●		●
Design a Back Cover	●			●		●	●		●	●	●	●	●